Homes@mnp

Written by **Kristin Gies** & **Peter Tonn** ● Illustrated by **Hannah Tews**

In memory of **Katy Juneau-Tews**

MEQUON *Nature Preserve*

Dragonfly

MNP is a home for many animals. Homes can be found high and low, and might even be hidden.

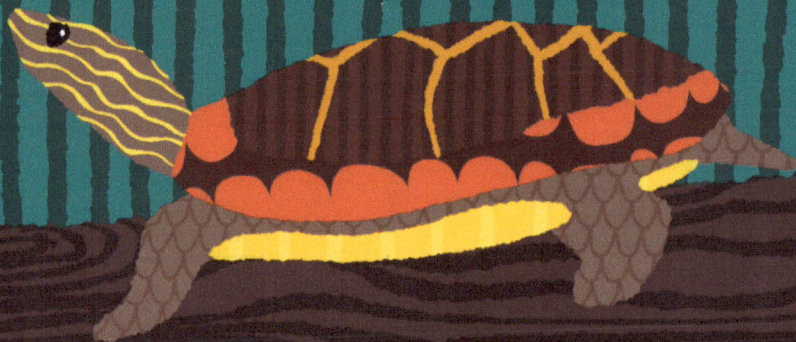

Painted Turtle

Kingfisher

SPRING POND

Leopard Frogs

Chipmunk

Sowbugs

Raccoon

HOLLOW LOG

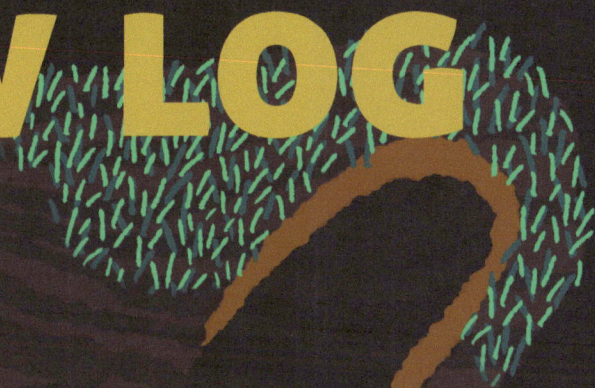

Monarch Butterfly

Bumble Bee

13-Lined Ground Squirrel

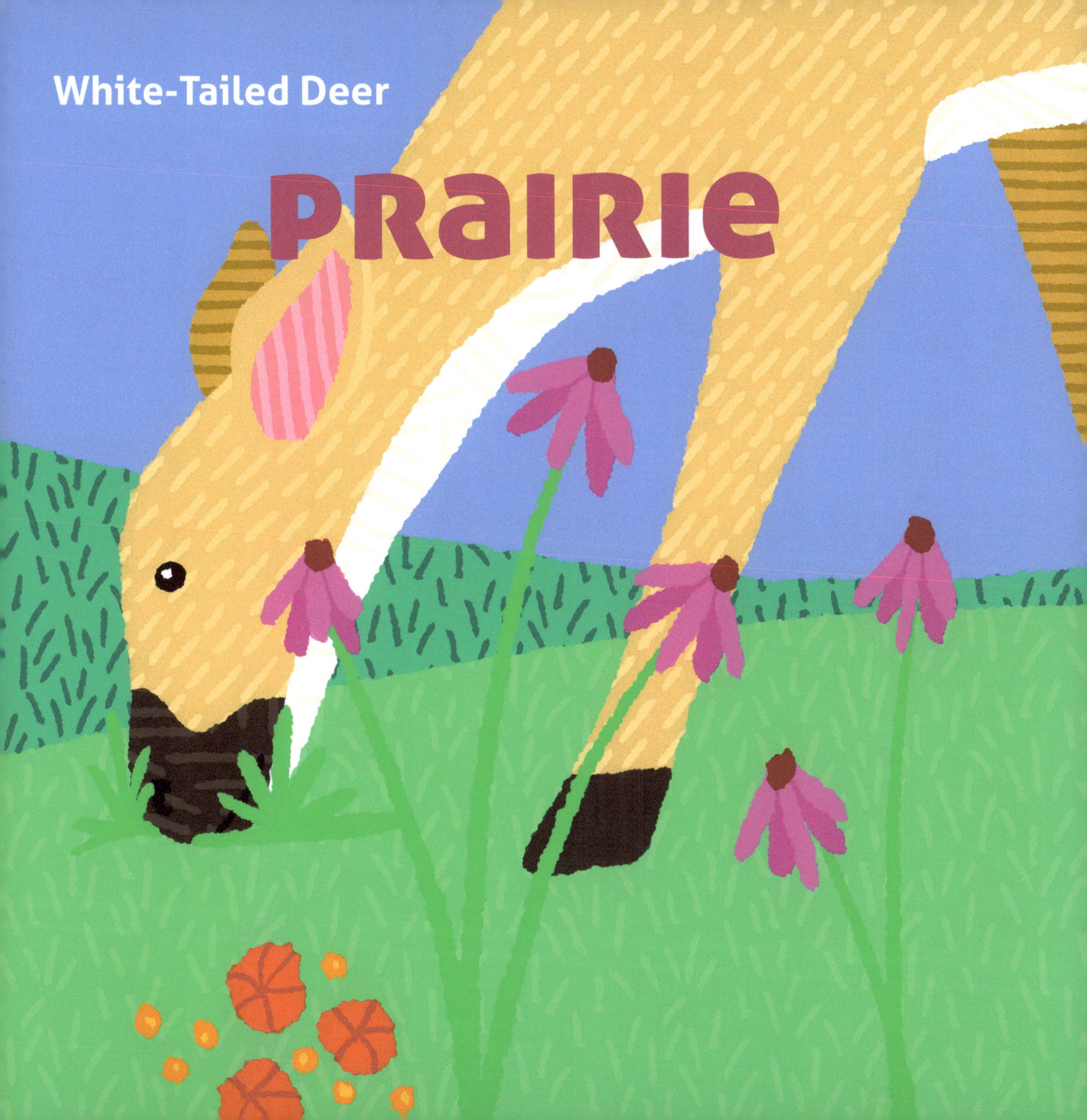

White-Tailed Deer

PRAIRIE

Crayfish

Mole

UNDERGROUND

Salamander

Fire Ants

Cardinal

Horned Owl

Flying Squirrels

FOREST

Pileated Woodpeckers

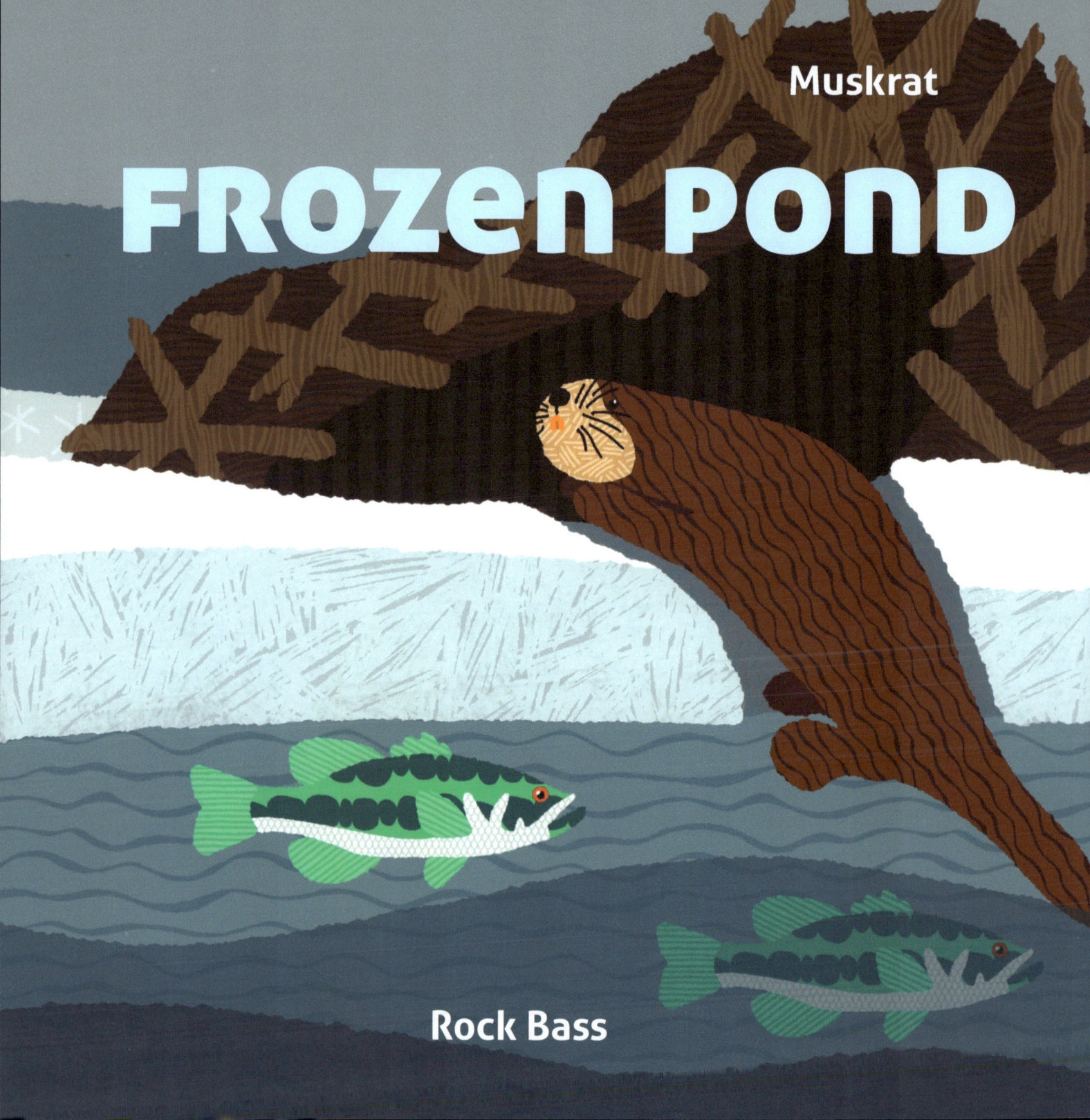

Muskrat

FROZEN POND

Rock Bass

Coyote

Tadpoles

SUBNIVEAN

Red Fox

Vole

Short-Tailed Weasel

Field Mouse

Bluebird House

Bat House

HOMeS@HOMe

Bee Apiary

Explore our trails to see which homes you can find. MNP trails are open to the public every day of the year, from sunrise to sunset, at no charge.

How many animals did you find in their homes today?

Mequon Nature Preserve is a 510-acre active land restoration site and living laboratory where you can explore, discover, breathe, learn and help restore 5 different ecosystems. There are no trail fees, no membership fees, just come enjoy, reconnect with the land and watch the transformation happen right before your eyes. Just 20 years into a 150-year restoration plan, 80,000 trees and shrubs have been planted. Thirty acres of wetland restored and hundreds of native wildlife and plant species are now thriving thanks to donors, community partners, and volunteers who all come together in concert to make this incredible transformation possible.

Published by Orange Hat Publishing 2024
HC ISBN: 9781645387756

orangehatpublishing.com

www.ingramcontent.com/pod-product-compliance
Lightning Source LLC
Chambersburg PA
CBHW042003100426
42813CB00020B/2970